English Tourism Council

Where to Stay in England 2000

Bed & Breakfast
Guest Accommodation

Official Guide to Assessed Accommodation

- Guesthouses
- Bed and Breakfast
- Farmhouses
- Inns

25th
ANNIVERSARY EDITION

Ratings you can trust

English Tourism Council

GUEST ACCOMMODATION

When you're looking for a place to stay, you need a rating system you can trust. The **English Tourism Council's** ratings are your clear guide to what to expect, in an easy-to-understand form. Properties are visited annually by our trained impartial assessors, so you can have confidence that your accommodation has been thoroughly checked and rated for quality before you make a booking.

Using a simple one to five Diamond rating, the new system puts a much greater emphasis on quality and is based on research which shows exactly what consumers are looking for when choosing accommodation.

"Guest Accommodation" covers a wide variety of serviced accommodation for which England is renowned, including guesthouses, bed and breakfasts, inns and farmhouses. Establishments are rated from one to five Diamonds. The same minimum requirement for facilities and services applies to all Guest Accommodation from one to five Diamonds. Progressively higher levels of quality and customer care must be provided for each of the one to five Diamond ratings. The rating reflects the unique character of Guest Accommodation, and covers areas such as cleanliness, service and hospitality, bedrooms, bathrooms and food quality.

Look out, too, for the English Tourism Council's new Gold and Silver Awards, which are awarded to those establishments which not only achieve the overall quality required for their Diamond rating, but also reach the highest levels of quality in those specific areas which guests identify as being really important for them. They will reflect the quality of comfort and cleanliness you'll find in the bedrooms and bathrooms and the quality of service you'll enjoy throughout your stay.

The new ratings are your sign of quality assurance, giving you the confidence to book the accommodation that meets your expectations.

Welcome

Bed & Breakfast
Guest Accommodation

Where to Stay
in England 2000

English Tourism Council

Changing Roles
The English Tourist Board becomes the English Tourism Council

The English Tourism Council is the national body for English Tourism. The ETC is funded by the Department for Culture, Media and Sport and was launched in July 1999 as a radical transformation of the existing English Tourist Board. Its role is to support the business of tourism and to drive forward a long-term vision for the industry. It will do this by working to improve the quality of England's tourism experience - for example, by working to increase standards in accommodation and service quality across the industry - to strengthen competitiveness and to encourage the wise growth of tourism. The ETC is a strategic body brokering partnerships, setting standards, developing policy, providing research and forecasts, and championing issues at the highest level.

Important:
The information contained in this guide has been published in good faith on the basis of information submitted to the English Tourism Council by the proprietors of the premises listed, who have paid for their entries to appear. The English Tourism Council cannot guarantee the accuracy of the information in this guide and accepts no responsibility for any error or misrepresentation. All liability for loss, disappointment, negligence or other damage caused by reliance on the information contained in this guide, or in the event of bankruptcy, or liquidation, or cessation of trade of any company, individual or firm mentioned, is hereby excluded. Please check carefully all prices and other details before confirming a reservation.

Cover Pictures:
Front Cover: (from top left)
The Bell Inn, Market Harborough, Leicestershire
Mariners, Sidmouth, Devon
Lains Cottage, Quarley, Hampshire
(Main Picture) Fields Farm, Alton, Staffordshire

Photo Credits:
Cumbria - Cumbria Tourist Board
Northumbria - Northumbria Tourist Board, Graeme Peacock, Mike Kipling, Colin Cuthbert and Michael Busselle
North West - North West Tourist Board, Cheshire County Council, Lancashire County Council, Marketing Manchester
Yorkshire - Yorkshire Tourist Board
Heart of England - Heart of England Tourist Board
East of England - East of England Tourist Board Collection
West Country - West Country Tourist Board
South of England - Southern Tourist Board, Peter Titmuss, Chris Cove-Smith and Iris Buckley
South East England - South East England Tourist Board, Chris Parker and Iris Buckley

Published by: The English Tourism Council, Thames Tower, Black's Road, Hammersmith, London W6 9EL.
ISBN 0 86143 212 6
Publishing Manager: Jane Collinson
Technical Manager: Marita Sen
Compilation & Production: Guide Associates, Croydon
Design: Jackson Lowe Marketing, Lewes, East Sussex
Typesetting: Tradespools Ltd, Somerset and Jackson Lowe Marketing, Lewes
Maps: ©Maps in Minutes™ (1999)
Printing and Binding: Jarrold Book Publishing, 3 Fison Way, Thetford, Norfolk IP24 1HT
Advertisement Sales: Madison Bell Ltd, 20 Orange Street, London WC2H 7ED. (020) 7389 0808.
© English Tourism Council (except where stated)

Contents
CONTENTS

WELCOME TO WHERE TO STAY
● How to find your way around the guide including colour maps

PLACES TO STAY AND THINGS TO DO
● Accommodation entries, places to visit, regional tourist board
contact details and travel to the area

FURTHER INFORMATION
● Detailed information on accommodation ratings,
guidance on how to book, events and more

KEY TO SYMBOLS
A key to symbols can be found on the inside back cover.
Keep it open for easy reference.

Welcome
WELCOME

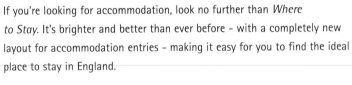

Welcome to our millennium
edition - it's so easy to use,
and packed with information.

If you're looking for accommodation, look no further than *Where to Stay*. It's brighter and better than ever before - with a completely new layout for accommodation entries - making it easy for you to find the ideal place to stay in England.

You'll also find

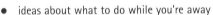

- ideas about what to do while you're away
- advice and information on booking your accommodation
- colour location maps
- local Tourist Information Centre telephone numbers
- information on events throughout the country

How to use
THE GUIDE

The guide is divided into the 10 English Regional Tourist Board regions (these are shown on page 14). Within these sections you will find a brief introduction to the area, contact details for the Regional Tourist Board, information about places to visit during your stay, and clear information entries on accommodation within the region. Accommodation is listed alphabetically in order of place name. If you would like to know more about the city, town or village in which you wish to stay, you will find brief descriptions at the end of each regional section. Or you can contact the local Tourist Information Centre - the telephone number can be found next to the town name on the accommodation entry pages.

Finding your ACCOMMODATION

Whether you know exactly where you want to stay or only have an idea of the area you wish to visit, it couldn't be easier to find accommodation to suit you in *Where to Stay*. You can find your accommodation in several ways:

by place
if you know the town or village look in the comprehensive **town index** at the back.

by area
if you know the area look at the **full colour maps** starting on page 16. All the places in purple offer accommodation featured in this guide.

by region
if you know which part of England look in the relevant **regional section**. These are colour coded at the top of each page. A map showing the regions can be found on page 14.

by county
if you know which English county look at the **county listing** on page 15 to find the region it is in.

You will also find a comprehensive accommodation listing (starting on page 555), which gives contact details of **all** guest accommodation which has been assessed by the English Tourism Council.

For help and advice about making a booking turn to the further information section at the back of the guide. It's all there to make finding and arranging your accommodation as easy as possible.

Types of ACCOMMODATION

Guest accommodation is featured in this guide which includes Guest Houses, Bed and Breakfast, Farmhouses and Inns.

Within each entry you will find a brief description of each property and facilities available.

(We publish a separate guide for hotel accommodation.)

Accommodation RATINGS & AWARDS

New ratings are your sign of quality assurance giving you the confidence to book accommodation that meets your expectations.

- The English Tourism Council's new Quality Assurance Scheme will help you find accommodation that really suits you. Based on new Diamond ratings, the Scheme provides you with reliable information about the quality of accommodation you can expect (see opposite). A Gold or Silver Award is given to establishments achieving the highest levels of quality within their Diamond rating. Turn to page 9 for a list of properties featured in the regional sections who have achieved a Gold Award.

- The England for Excellence awards run by the English Tourism Council also represent the highest level of tourism standards and details of nominees and winners can be found on page 13.

- If access to accommodation is an important criteria because you are a wheelchair user or have difficulty walking, please look on pages 10 and 11. You will find a list of establishments who participate in the National Accessible Scheme.

English Tourism Council

◆ ◆ ◆
GUEST ACCOMMODATION

MAKING A BOOKING

Please remember that changes may occur after the guide is printed. When you have found a suitable place to stay we advise you to contact the establishment to check availability, and also to confirm prices and any specific facilities which may be important to you. Further advice on how to make a booking can be found at the back of this guide, together with information about deposits and cancellations. When you have made your booking, if you have time, it is advisable to confirm it in writing.

RATINGS YOU CAN TRUST

When you're looking for a place to stay, you need a rating system you can trust. The English Tourism Council's ratings give a clear guide to what to expect, in an easy-to-understand form. Properties are visited annually by trained, impartial assessors, so you can have the confidence that your accommodation has been thoroughly checked and rated for quality before you make your booking.

Diamond ratings

Ratings are awarded from one to five Diamonds. The more Diamonds, the higher the quality and the greater the range of facilities and level of service provided. The brief explanations of the Diamond ratings outlined here show what is included at each rating level (note that each rating also includes what is provided at a lower Diamond rating).

◆ Clean accommodation, providing acceptable comfort and quality with functional decor and a helpful service. As a minimum, a full cooked or continental breakfast is provided. Other meals, if prepared, will be freshly cooked. Towels are provided and heating and hot water will be available as reasonable times.

◆◆ A sound overall level of quality and customer care in all areas.

◆◆◆ A good overall level of quality in areas such as comfortable bedrooms, well maintained, practical decor, the choice of items at breakfast, customer care and all-round comfort. Where other meals are provided these will be freshly cooked from good quality ingredients.

◆◆◆◆ A very good level of quality in all areas. Customer care showing very good attention to your needs.

◆◆◆◆◆ An excellent overall level of quality - for example, ample space with a degree of luxury, a high quality bed and furniture, excellent interior design and customer care which anticipates your needs. Breakfast offering a wide choice of high quality fresh ingredients. Where other meals are provided these will feature fresh, seasonal, local ingredients.

Gold and Silver Awards

Look out too, for the Gold and Silver Awards which are exclusive to the English Tourism Council. They are awarded to those establishments which not only achieve the overall quality required for their Diamond rating, but also reach the highest level of quality in those specific areas which guests identify as being really important for them. They will reflect the quality of comfort and cleanliness you will find in the bedrooms and bathroom and the quality of service you'll enjoy throughout your stay.

Accommodation dation
ENTRIES EXPLAINED

Each accommodation entry contains detailed information to help you decide if it is right for you. This information has been provided by the proprietors themselves, and our aim has been to ensure that it is as objective and factual as possible. Below the establishment name you will find the Diamond rating and quality award, if appropriate.

At-a-glance symbols at the end of each entry give you additional information on services and facilities - a key can be found on the back cover flap. Keep this open to refer to as you read.

A sample entry is shown below.

Sample Entry

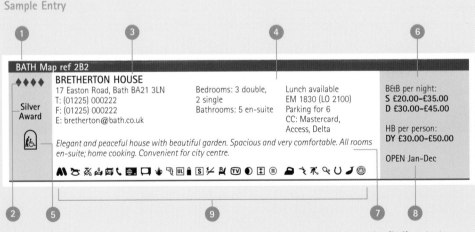

BATH Map ref 2B2		
♦♦♦♦ Silver Award	**BRETHERTON HOUSE** 17 Easton Road, Bath BA21 3LN T: (01225) 000222 F: (01225) 000222 E: bretherton@bath.co.uk	Bedrooms: 3 double, 2 single Bathrooms: 5 en-suite

Lunch available
EM 1830 (LO 2100)
Parking for 6
CC: Mastercard,
Access, Delta

B&B per night:
S £20.00–£35.00
D £30.00–£45.00

HB per person:
DY £30.00–£50.00

OPEN Jan-Dec

Elegant and peaceful house with beautiful garden. Spacious and very comfortable. All rooms en-suite; home cooking. Convenient for city centre.

1   Town or village with map reference

2   Diamond rating and quality award (where applicable)

3   Establishment name, address and contact details

4   Accommodation details, including credit cards accepted

5   National Accessible Scheme rating (where applicable)

6   Prices per night for bed & breakfast (B&B) staying in a single (S) or double (D) room. The double room price is for two people. Half board (HB) prices are shown as a daily rate (DY) per person and include room, breakfast and dinner

7   Accommodation description

8   Months open

9   At-a-glance symbols (key on back cover flap)

8

GOLD

Gold Award

Award Establishments

Guest accommodation featured in the regional sections of this *Where to Stay* guide which have achieved a Gold Award for an exceptionally high standard of quality are listed on this page. Please use the Town Index at the back of the guide to find the page numbers for their full entry listings.

For further information about Gold Awards, please see page 7.

The Barn, Pershore, Worcestershire
Blounts Court Farm, Devizes, Wiltshire
Bokiddick Farm, Bodmin, Cornwall
Broadview Gardens, Crewkerne, Somerset
Burhill Farm, Broadway, Worcestershire
Buxton's Victorian Guesthouse, Buxton, Derbyshire
Chalon House, Richmond, London
Cloud High, Barnard Castle, Durham
Coniston Lodge, Coniston, Cumbria
Cotteswold House, Bibury, Gloucestershire
The Cottage, Bishop's Stortford, Hertfordshire
East End House, Fairfold, Gloucestershire
Efford Cottage, Lymington, Hampshire
Folly Farm Cottage, Stratford-upon-Avon, Warwickshire
Greenwood Lodge City Guesthouse, Nottingham, Nottinghamshire
Hotel Number Sixteen, London SW7
Hooke Hall, Uckfield, East Sussex
Kimmeridge Farmhouse, Kimmeridge, Dorset
Lavenham Priory, Lavenham, Suffolk
Leighton House, Bath, Bath & North East Somerset
Lichfield Guest House, Ashbourne, Derbyshire
Magnolia House, Canterbury, Kent
The Manor, Linton, Derbyshire
Manor Farm Oast, Rye, East Sussex
Manorhouse, Bury St Edmonds, Suffolk
Meadowland, Bath, Bath & North East Somerset
Nonsuch House, Dartmouth, Devon
The Nurse's Cottage, Sway, Hampshire
The Old Tump House, Blakeney, Gloucestershire
The Ringlestone Inn & Farmhouse Hotel, Maidstone, Kent
Rosefield House, Lymington, Hampshire
Seaham Guest House, Weymouth, Dorset
Shipton Glebe, Woodstock, Oxfordshire
Stonebank, Chickerell, Dorset
Tavern House, Tetbury, Gloucestershire
Thanington Hotel, Canterbury, Kent
Thatch Lodge Hotel, Lyme Regis, Dorset
Tor Cottage, Tavistock, Devon
Villa Magdala Hotel, Bath, Bath & North East Somerset

The Pictures:
1 Tor Cottage,
   Tavistock, Devon;
2 Lavenham Priory,
   Lavenham, Suffolk;
3 Thanington Hotel,
   Canterbury, Kent.

National
ACCESSIBLE SCHEME

The English Tourism Council and National and Regional Tourist Boards throughout Britain assess all types of places to stay, on holiday or business, that provide accessible accommodation for wheelchair users and others who may have difficulty walking.

Accommodation establishments taking part in the National Accessible Scheme, and which appear in the regional sections of this guide are listed opposite. Use the Town Index at the back to find the page numbers for their full entries.

The Tourist Boards recognise three categories of accessibility:

 CATEGORY 1   Accessible to all wheelchair users including those travelling independently.

 CATEGORY 2   Accessible to a wheelchair user with assistance.

 CATEGORY 3   Accessible to a wheelchair user able to walk short distances and up at least three steps.

If you have additional needs or special requirements of any kind, we strongly recommend that you make sure these can be met by your chosen establishment before you confirm your booking.

The criteria that the English Tourism Council and National and Regional Tourist Boards have adopted do not necessarily conform to British Standards or to Building Regulations. They reflect what the Boards understand to be acceptable to meet the practical needs of wheelchair users.

The National Accessible Scheme forms part of the Tourism for All Campaign that is being promoted by the English Tourism Council and all National and Regional Tourist Boards. Additional help and guidance on finding suitable holiday accommodation for those with special needs can be obtained from:

Holiday Care Service,
2nd Floor, Imperial Buildings,
Victoria Road,
Horley,
Surrey RH6 7PZ

Tel: (01293) 774535
Fax: (01293) 784647
Minicom: (01293) 776943

 CATEGORY 1

- Alkmonkton, Derbyshire - The Courtyard
- Crookham, Northumberland
  - The Coach House at Crookham
- Farnham, Surrey - High Wray
- Selsey, West Sussex - St Andrews Lodge
- Telford, Shropshire - Old Rectory
- Wells, Somerset - Burcott Mill Guest House
- Wilmslow, Cheshire - Dean Bank Hotel
- Woodbridge, Suffolk - Grove House
- Worthing, West Sussex - The Lantern Hotel

 CATEGORY 2

- Castle Donington, Leicestershire
  - Donington Park Farmhouse Hotel
- Devizes, Wiltshire - Longwater
- Ireby, Cumbria - Woodlands Country House
- Southport, Merseyside - Sandy Brook Farm

CATEGORY 3

- Ambleside, Cumbria
  - Borrans Park Hotel
  - Rowanfield Country Guesthouse
- Arundel, West Sussex - Mill Lane House
- Ashburton, Devon - New Cott Farm
- Bakewell, Derbyshire - Tannery House

- Boscastle, Cornwall - The Old Coach House
- Bratton Fleming, Devon
  - Bracken House Country Hotel
- Bridgnorth, Shropshire - Bulls Head Inn
- Colyton, Devon - Smallicombe Farm
- Congleton, Cheshire - Sandhole Farm
- Cressbrook, Derbyshire - Cressbrook Hall
- Earls Colne, Essex - Riverside Lodge
- Fareham, Hampshire - Avenue House Hotel
- Frome, Somerset - Fourwinds Guest Hotel
- Gosport, Hampshire - West Wind Guest House
- Henley-on-Thames, Oxfordshire - Holmwood
- Ingleton, North Yorkshire - Riverside Lodge
- Lenham, Kent - The Dog and Bear Hotel
- Lower Whitley, Cheshire - Tall Trees Lodge
- Lymington, Hampshire - Our Bench
- Northallerton, North Yorkshire
  - Lovesome Hill Farm
- Norwich, Norfolk - Elm Farm Country House
- Okehampton, Devon - Week Farm
- Oxford, Oxfordshire - Acorn Guest House
- Redcar, Tees Valley - Falcon Hotel
- Richmond, North Yorkshire - Mount Pleasant Farm
- Salisbury, Wiltshire - Byways House
- Sandbach, Cheshire
  - Canal Centre and Village Store
- Sarre, Kent
  - Crown Inn (The Famous Cherry Brandy House)
- Skipton, North Yorkshire - Craven Heifer Inn
- Stratford-upon-Avon, Warwickshire - Church Farm
- Sway, Hampshire - The Nurse's Cottage
- Threlkeld, Cumbria
  - Scales Farm Country Guesthouse
- Weston-super-Mare, North Somerset
  - Moorlands Country Guesthouse
- Whitley Bay, Tyne & Wear
  - Marlborough Hotel
  - York House Hotel
- Winchester, Hampshire - Shawlands

(The information contained on these pages was correct at the time of going to press.)

11

RASOOL COURT HOTEL

**19-21 Penywern Road,
Earls Court, London, SW5 9TT
Tel: 020 7373 8900 Fax: 020 7244 6835
Email: rasool@rasool.demon.co.uk
Web site: www.rasoolcourthotel.com**

*Single from £34, Double from £46, Triple from £62, Family from £79.
For best rate and location. Open 24 hours, most rooms with private showers.
All rooms with colour TV's, Sky Movies & Sport Channels and telephones.*

The Rasool Court Hotel is a family run hotel with 57 bedrooms. The hotel itself is ideally located in fashionable Kensington, close to the heart of the city. Within one minutes walk from Earls Court station which makes most major shopping areas of Knightsbridge, Oxford Street and tourist attraction of Buckingham Palace, The Tower of London and the museums with easy reach.

The immediate area itself has variety of restaurant and shops for your convenience.

RAMSEES HOTEL

**32/36 Hogarth Road
Earls Court, London, SW5 0PU
Tel: 020 7370 1445
Fax: 020 7244 6835
Email: ramsees@rasool.demon.co.uk
Web site: www.ramseeshotel.com**

*Single from £29, Double from £41, Triple from £66, Family from £75.
For best rate and location. Open 24 hours, most rooms with private showers.
All rooms with colour TV's, Sky Movies & Sport Channels and telephones.*

The hotel itself is ideally located in the heart of the city. Within one minutes walk from Earls Court station, which makes most major shopping areas and tourist attractions like Buckingham Palace, The Tower of London, Knightsbridge, Oxford Street, Piccadilly and the museums within easy reach.

The immediate area itself has variety of restaurant and shops for your convenience.

The ENGLAND FOR EXCELLENCE
Awards 1999

ENGLAND FOR
EXCELLENCE
AWARDS 1999

La creme de la creme

If you are looking for somewhere truly outstanding, then why not try one of the following B&Bs listed below. Having proved their mettle at a regional level, each one has made it through to the semi-finals of the 1999 England for Excellence Awards. Run by the English Tourism Council in association with the Regional Tourist Boards, these highly competitive annual awards reward only the very best in English tourism. So if somewhere has made it through to the short-list, you can be sure that they really are the bees knees.

Sponsored by:

Number Thirty One, Howard Place, Carlisle `WINNER`	**Tel: 01228 597080**
The Priory, Lavenham, Suffolk `SILVER`	**Tel: 01787 247404**
The Old Bakery, Blockley, Moreton-in-Marsh, Gloucestershire (joint regional winner)	**Tel: 01386 700408**
Upper Brompton Farm, Cross Houses, Shrewsbury, Shropshire (joint regional winner)	**Tel: 01743 761629**
Five Sumner Place Hotel, South Kensington, London	**Tel: 020 7584 7586**
The Old Manse, Charlton Alnwick, Northumbria	**Tel: 01668 215343**
The Old Coach House, Blackpool	**Tel: 01253 349195**
Number One Lime Chase, Storrington, West Sussex `SILVER`	**Tel: 01903 740437**
Shipton Glebe, Woodstock, Oxfordshire	**Tel: 01993 812688**
The Old Bakehouse, Chulmleigh, Devon	**Tel: 01769 580074**
Helm, Askrigg, North Yorkshire	**Tel: 01969 650443**

Regional TOURIST BOARD Areas

This *Where to Stay* guide is divided into 10 regional sections as shown on the map below. To identify each regional section and its page number, please refer to the key below. The county index on the opposite page indicates in which regional section you will find a particular county.

Each of the ten English regions shown here has a Regional Tourist Board which can give you information about things to see or do locally. Contact details are given both at the beginning and end of each regional section.

Location Maps

Colour location maps showing all the cities, towns and villages with accommodation in the regional sections of this guide can be found on pages 16 - 28. Turn to the Town Index at the back of this guide for the page number on which you can find the relevant accommodation.

In which region is the county
I WISH TO VISIT?

COUNTY/UNITARY AUTHORITY	REGION
Bath & North East Somerset	West Country
Bedfordshire	East of England
Berkshire	South of England
Bristol	West Country
Buckinghamshire	South of England
Cambridgeshire	East of England
Cheshire	North West
Cornwall	West Country
Cumbria	Cumbria
Derbyshire	Heart of England
Derbyshire High Peak District	North West
Devon	West Country
Dorset (Eastern)	South of England
Dorset (Western)	West Country
Durham	Northumbria
East Riding of Yorkshire	Yorkshire
East Sussex	South East England
Essex	East of England
Gloucestershire	Heart of England
Greater London	London
Greater Manchester	North West
Hampshire	South of England
Herefordshire	Heart of England
Hertfordshire	East of England
Isle of Wight	South of England
Isles of Scilly	West Country
Kent	South East England
Lancashire	North West
Leicestershire	Heart of England
Lincolnshire	East of England
Merseyside	North West
Norfolk	East of England
North East Lincolnshire	Yorkshire
North Lincolnshire	Yorkshire
North Somerset	West Country
North Yorkshire	Yorkshire
Northamptonshire	Heart of England
Northumberland	Northumbria
Nottinghamshire	Heart of England
Oxfordshire	South of England
Rutland	Heart of England
Shropshire	Heart of England
Somerset	West Country
South Gloucestershire	West Country
South Yorkshire	Yorkshire
Staffordshire	Heart of England
Suffolk	East of England
Surrey	South East England
Tees Valley	Northumbria
Tyne & Wear	Northumbria
Warwickshire	Heart of England
West Midlands	Heart of England
West Sussex	South East England
West Yorkshire	Yorkshire
Wiltshire	West Country
Worcestershire	Heart of England
York	Yorkshire

UNITARY AUTHORITIES

Please note that many new unitary authorities have been formed - for example Brighton & Hove and Bristol - and are officially separate from the county in which they were previously located. To aid the reader we have only included the major unitary authorities in the list above and on the colour maps.

MAP 1

Location MAPS

Every place name featured in the regional accommodation sections of this Where to Stay guide has a map reference to help you locate it on the maps which follow. For example, to find Colchester, Essex, which has 'Map ref 3B2', turn to Map 3 and refer to grid square B2.

All place names appearing in the regional sections are shown in purple type on the maps. This enables you to find other places in your chosen area which may have suitable accommodation - the Town Index (at the back of this guide) gives page numbers.

MAP 5
Newcastle upon Tyne
Carlisle

MAP 4
York
Manchester
Lincoln

Birmingham
Ipswich

MAP 2
Oxford
Bristol
Southampton

MAPS 6&7
London

MAP 1

Dover

MAP 3

Exeter

Boscastle
Tintagel
A39
St Kew
Padstow
Wadebridge
St Mawgan
Watergate Bay
NEWQUAY
Bodmin
A38
Newquay
A392
A30
CORNWALL
A391
Perranporth
A30
St Austell
St Agnes
Goonhavern
A39
Fowey
A390
Grampound
Truro
A3078
Mevagissey
St Ives
A30
A390
Hayle
A394
Pendeen
St Just-in-Penwith
Penzance
A394
Helston
Falmouth
A30
Mawgan
ISLES OF SCILLY
Mullion
A3083
Isles of Scilly
(St. Mary's)
Lizard

MAP 1

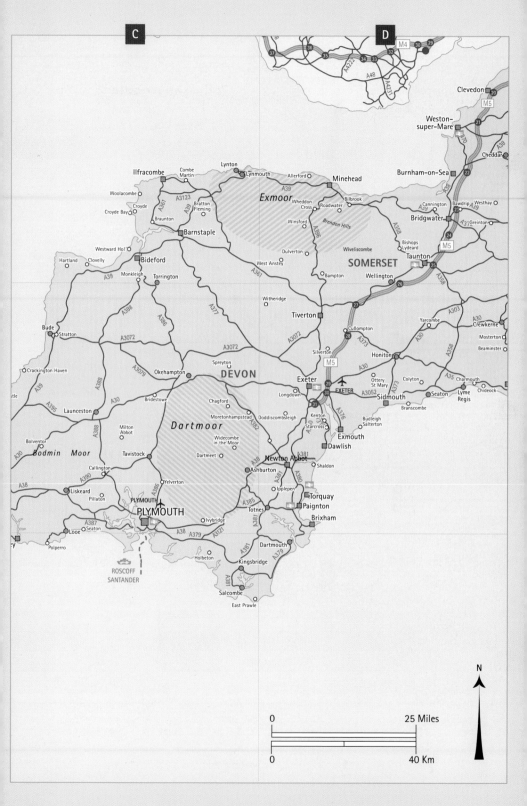

MAP 2

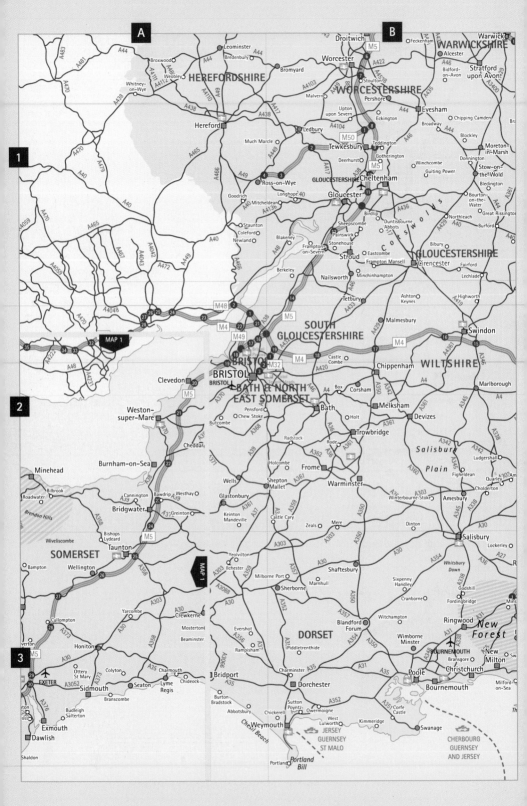

MAP 2

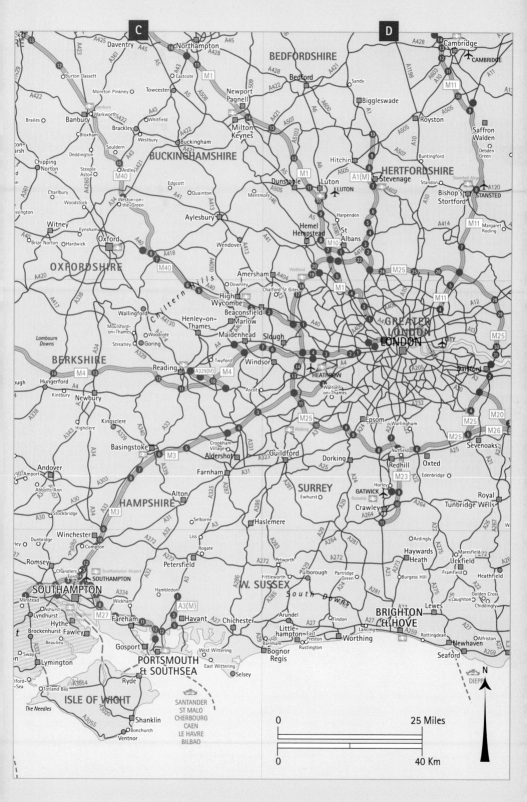

MAP 3

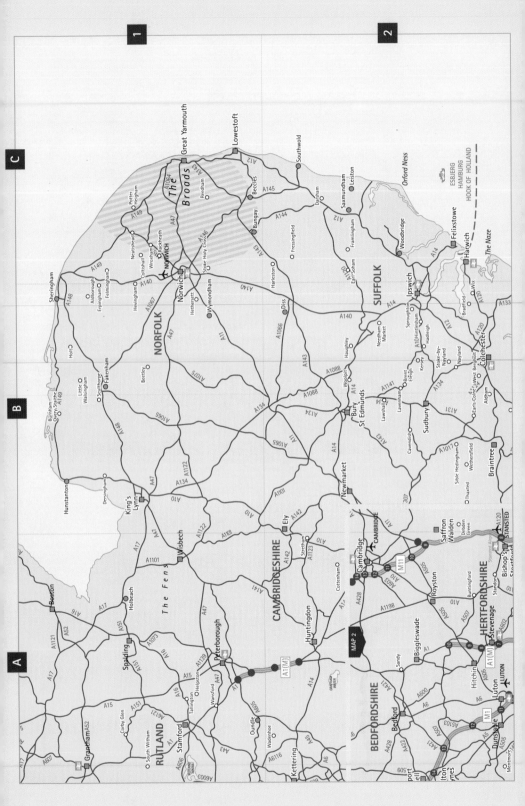

C

Great Yarmouth
Lowestoft
The Broads
Southwold
Potter Heigham
Reedham
Beccles
A149
A47
Bungay
A144
A145
Leiston
Saxmundham
Darsham
Orford Ness
ESBJERG
HAMBURG
HOOK OF HOLLAND
Neatishead
Wroxham
Rackheath
Coltishall
Stoke Holy Cross
Fressingfield
Framlingham
Woodbridge
Felixstowe
Harwich
The Naze
A146
Sheringham
A148
Aldborough
Erpingham
Felmingham
Hevingham
NORWICH
Norwich
Hethersett
Wymondham
Harleston
A140
A140
Earl Soham
Sproughton
A10
A10 Hintlesham
Ipswich
Bramford
A14
A120
A133
Holt
B
NORFOLK
A47
A140
A11
Diss
A1066
A143
Haughley
Needham Market
Hadleigh
Stoke-by-Nayland
Nayland
A134
Colchester
Little Walsingham
Beetley
Fakenham
Scoulthorpe
A1075
A1088
A1088
A134
A134
Woolpit
A14
A1141
Lavenham
Brent Eleigh
Kersey
Sudbury
Earls Colne
West Bergholt
A131
Burnham Overy Staithe
A149
A148
A1065
A11
Bury St Edmunds
A142
Cavendish
Lawshall
Silke Hedingham
Wethersfield
Braintree
A1017
Hunstanton
Dersingham
A47
A1122
A134
A11
A14
Newmarket
Thaxted
King's Lynn
A10
A1101
Wisbech
A1122
Ely
A142
A142
A10
A10
Stretham
A123
Cottenham
CAMBRIDGESHIRE
CAMBRIDGE
Cambridge
Saffron Walden
Debden Green
STANSTED
A120
Bishop's Stortford
HERTFORDSHIRE
Royston
Buntingford
Standon
A
Boston
A16
A17
A52
A121
A151
Holbeach
The Fens
A47
A141
Huntingdon
A14
A428
A1198
A10
A507
Biggleswade
Stevenage
A1(M)
A602
Spalding
A151
A1073
A16
Peterborough
A1(M)
A14
Sandy
A1
Hitchin
LUTON
Luton
M1
Grantham
A52
Corby Glen
South Witham
A15
A16
Helpston
A1139
A47
Wansford
Tallington
Bedford
A428
A422
A421
A6
A600
Dunstable
A5
A505
A52
A607
A1
A606
Stamford
RUTLAND
Oundle
Wadenhoe
A43
A605
A6116
A45
A6
BEDFORDSHIRE
A421
A505
A5103
M1
A17
Kettering
port
ell
lton
nes
509
605
MAP 2

MAP 3

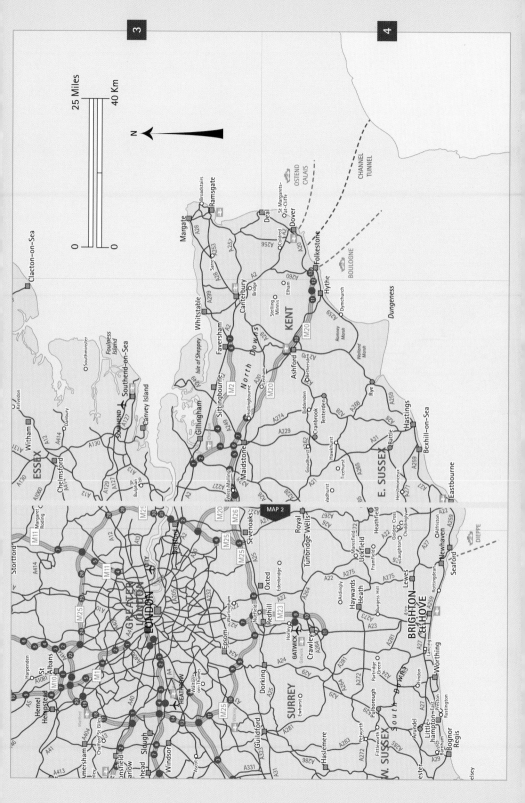

MAP 4

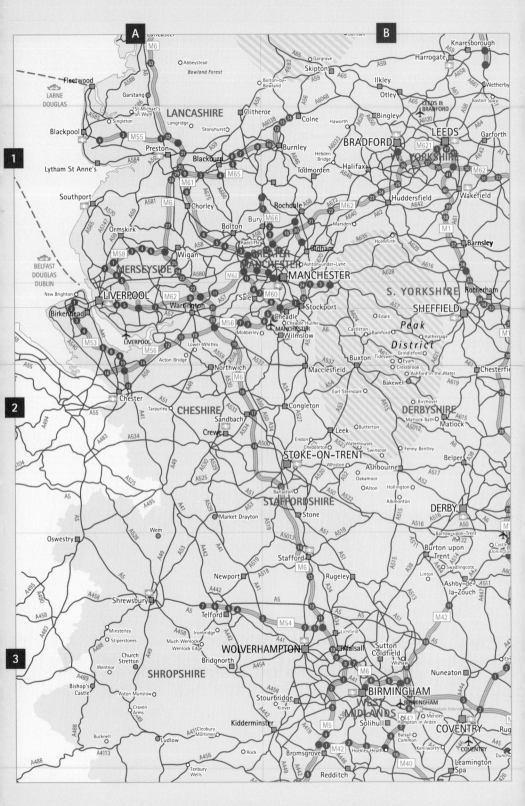

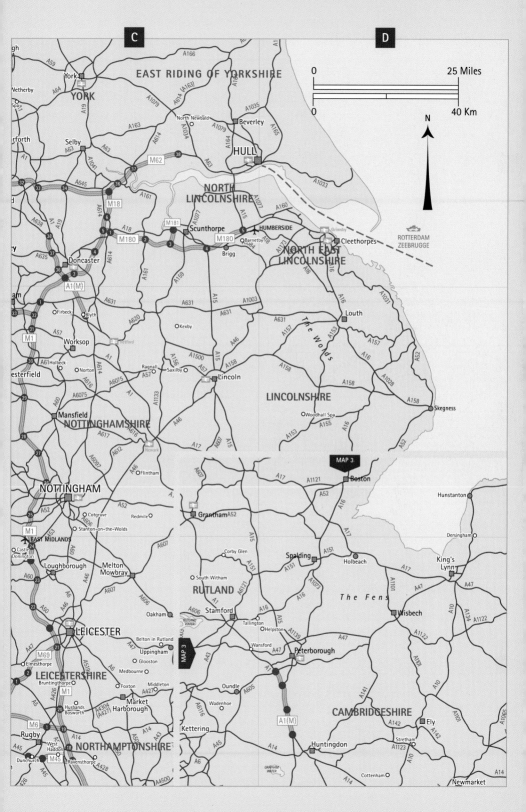

MAP 4

C

D

EAST RIDING OF YORKSHIRE

A166

York
YORK
A59
A64
A19
Wetherby
Spa
A614 (A163)
A1079
A164
A1035
North Newbald
A1079
Beverley
A163
A614
A165

HULL

Selby
A63
A1041
M62
38
37
36
NORTH
LINCOLNSHIRE
A1077
A63
A15
A1073
A160
A1033
A161
M18
6
M181
Scunthorpe
M180
5
HUMBERSIDE
Grimsby
Cleetorpes
ROTTERDAM
ZEEBRUGGE
M180
2
3
4
Barnetby
178
A18
A161
Brigg
NORTH EAST
LINCOLNSHIRE
A18
A16
Doncaster
A1(M)
A631
A631
A631
A15
A1003
A16
A1031
Louth
A153
A52
A57
Worksop
A1
A614
A46
A15
A158
A157
The Wolds
A16
A158
A158
A1028
Lincoln
A158
Skegness
A607
A15
A153
A155
A16
LINCOLNSHIRE
Woodhall Spa

NOTTINGHAM
A52
A17
MAP 3
Boston
A1121
A52
A16
Hunstanton
Grantham
A52
Dersingham
A151
King's
Lynn
Spalding
A151
Holbeach
A47
The Fens
RUTLAND
Stamford
A16
Wisbech
Peterborough
A47
LEICESTER
Uppingham
Oundle
A1(M)
CAMBRIDGESHIRE
Ely
Kettering
NORTHAMPTONSHIRE
Huntingdon
Newmarket

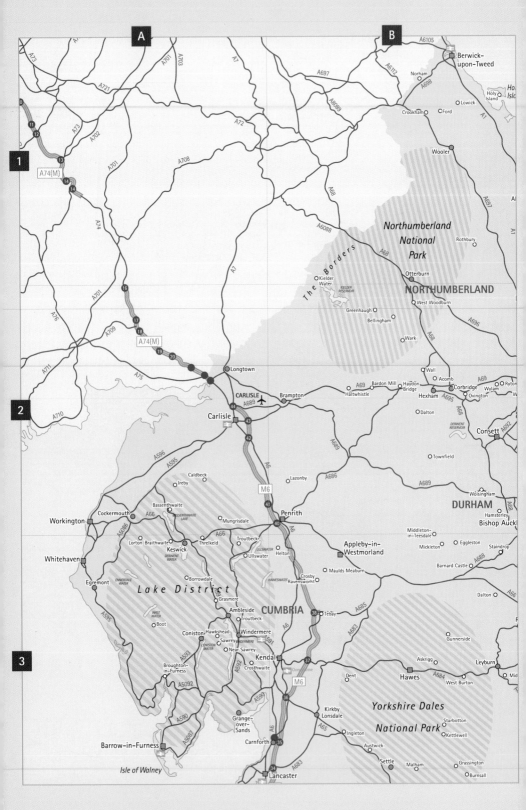

MAP 5

24

MAP 5

C

D

Holy Island

Farne Islands

Seahouses

Embleton
Craster

Alnwick
Lesbury
Alnmouth
Warkworth

A1
A1068

Morpeth

A1

A19
Whitley Bay
NEWCASTLE
Tynemouth
Ryton
NEWCASTLE UPON TYNE
Whickham
TYNE
& WEAR
Gateshead
SUNDERLAND

0   25 Miles

0   40 Km

N

BERGEN
STAVANGER
KIRSTIANSAND
HAUGESUND
AMSTERDAM (Ijmulden)
GOTHENBURG
HAMBURG

A692
A963
65
64
63
Chester-le-Street
A691
62
A19
Durham

A167
61

A68
Spennymoor
A1(M)
60
Auckland
A689
A689
A19
Hartlepool

Heighington
59
Stockton-on-Tees
TEES VALLEY
Redcar
Piercebridge
Middlesbrough
Darlington
TEESSIDE
Cleasby
57
Runswick
A66
56
Stokesley
A172
Danby
Whitby
Richmond
A167
A19
NORTH YORKS MOORS
Goathland
Robin Hood's Bay
Ravenscar
A169
Staintondale
NATIONAL PARK
Harwood Dale
Northallerton
A684
A168
Stape
North York Moors
A171
Middleham Bedale
A167
Levisham
Gillamoor
Cropton
Scarborough
A6108
Kirkbymoorside
Thirsk
Helmsley
A170
Pickering
Filey
Masham
Kirklington
A170
Ampleforth
Thornton Dale
A165
NORTH
YORKSHIRE
A19
Slingsby
Ripon
Malton
A1(M)
Boroughbridge
A64
Sledmere
Rudston A166
Bridlington
A61
A614
A165

25

MAP 6

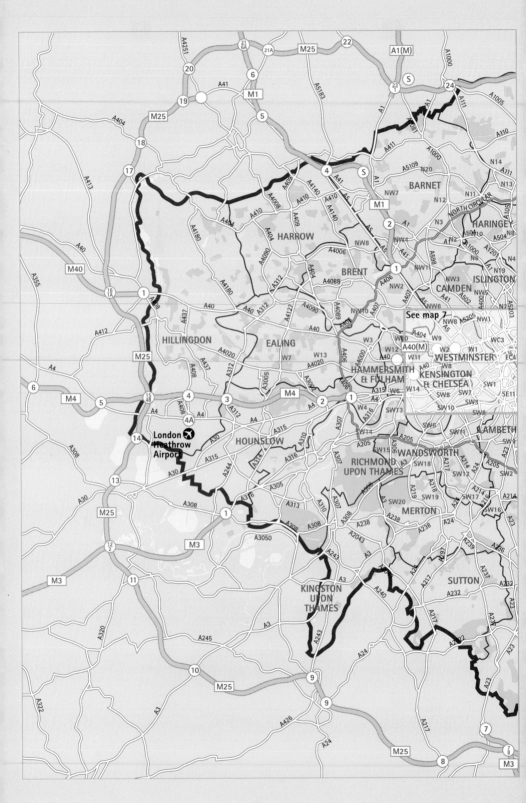

MAP 6

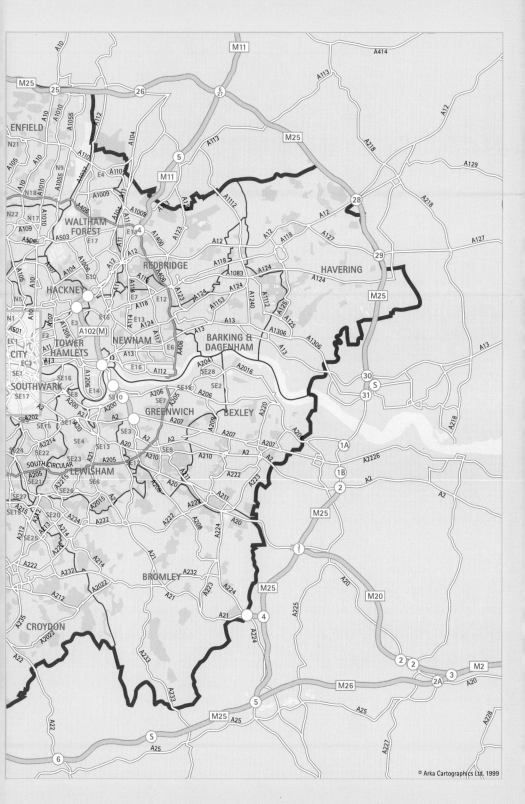

MAP 7

Central London

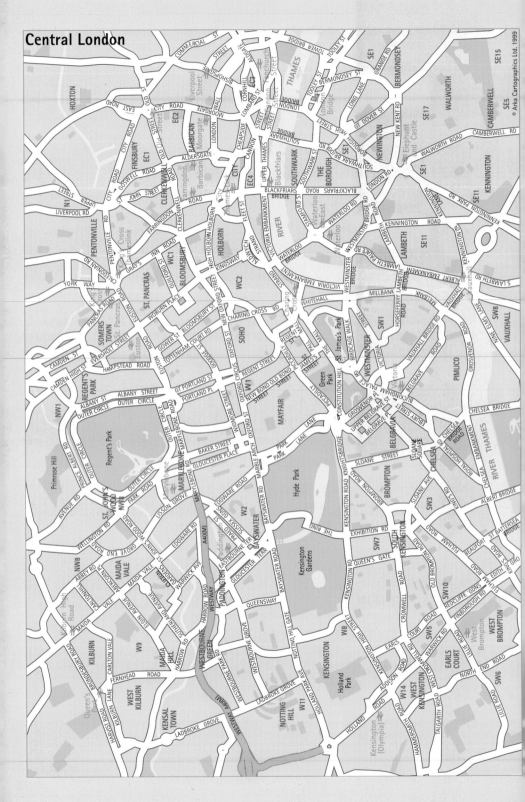

© Arka Cartographics Ltd. 1999